Best-Loved Chilis

Table of Contents

Chunky Black Bean and Sweet Potato Chili

2 teaspoons vegetable oil

1 cup chopped sweet onion

2 red or green bell peppers or 1 of each, cut into ½-inch chunks

4 cloves garlic, minced

1 teaspoon chili powder

1 can (about 14 ounces) fire-roasted diced tomatoes

1 small sweet potato (8 ounces), peeled and cut into ½-inch chunks

1 tablespoon minced chipotle chiles in adobo*

1 can (about 15 ounces) black beans, rinsed and drained

½ cup chopped fresh cilantro or green onions (optional)

Purée the contents of a 7-ounce can of chiles in a blender. Refrigerate or freeze remaining puréed chiles for another use.

1. Heat oil in large saucepan over medium heat. Add onion; cook and stir 5 minutes. Add bell peppers, garlic and chili powder; cook and stir 2 minutes.

2. Add tomatoes, sweet potato and chipotle chiles; bring to a boil. Cover and simmer over medium-low heat 15 minutes. Stir in beans; cover and simmer 8 to 10 minutes or until vegetables are tender. (Chili will be thick; thin with water as desired.)

3. Ladle into shallow bowls; top with cilantro or green onions, if desired.

Makes 4 servings

Chili Mac

1 pound ground beef or turkey
1 medium onion, chopped
1 green bell pepper, chopped
1 can (14½ ounces) Mexican or chili-style stewed tomatoes, undrained
½ cup water
1 package (1¼ ounces) taco seasoning mix
2 cups (7 ounces) elbow macaroni or small shells, cooked and drained
2 cups (8 ounces) SARGENTO® Shredded Reduced Fat 4 Cheese Mexican Cheese, divided

1. Cook ground beef, onion and green pepper in large skillet over medium heat 5 minutes or until beef is no longer pink; pour off drippings. Add tomatoes, water and taco seasoning; simmer 5 minutes, stirring occasionally.

2. Toss pasta with meat mixture. Spoon 3 cups of mixture into an 11×7-inch baking dish. Sprinkle with 1 cup cheese; top with remaining meat mixture. Cover with foil; bake in preheated 375°F oven 30 minutes. Uncover; sprinkle with remaining cheese. Return to oven 5 minutes or until cheese is melted. *Makes 6 servings*

Prep Time: 20 minutes
Cook Time: 35 minutes

Fresh Tomato Chili

    1 tablespoon olive oil
    1 small onion, chopped
    1 clove garlic, minced
    1 medium tomato, diced
    1 cup frozen corn
    1 can (about 15 ounces) kidney beans, rinsed and drained
    1 can (8 ounces) tomato sauce
    $\frac{1}{2}$ to $\frac{2}{3}$ cup reduced-sodium chicken or vegetable broth
    1 teaspoon chili powder
    $\frac{1}{2}$ teaspoon ground cumin
    $\frac{1}{4}$ teaspoon dried oregano
    $\frac{1}{8}$ teaspoon salt
    $\frac{1}{8}$ teaspoon black pepper
    $\frac{1}{8}$ teaspoon red pepper flakes
    1 cup water
    1 cup instant brown rice

1. Heat oil in large saucepan over medium-high heat. Add onion and garlic; cook and stir 5 minutes. Add tomato and corn; cook and stir 2 minutes.

2. Add beans, tomato sauce, $\frac{1}{2}$ cup broth, chili powder, cumin, oregano, salt, black pepper and red pepper flakes; simmer 6 to 8 minutes. Add additional broth if chili is too thick.

3. Meanwhile, bring water to a boil in small saucepan. Reduce heat to low. Add rice; cover and simmer 5 minutes. Remove from heat; let stand 5 minutes. Fluff with fork. Serve chili over rice.   *Makes 4 servings*

Texas Cowboy Chili

- 1 tablespoon vegetable oil
- 1 beef sirloin steak or boneless beef top round steak, cut into cubes (about 1 pound)
- 1 medium onion, chopped (about ½ cup)
- 1 small green pepper, chopped (about ½ cup)
- 1 teaspoon ground cumin
- 1 tablespoon all-purpose flour
- 1 cup PACE® Picante Sauce
- 1¾ cups SWANSON® Beef Broth or SWANSON® Beef Stock
  Assorted Toppers

1. Heat the oil in a 4-quart nonstick saucepan over medium-high heat. Add the beef and cook until it's well browned, stirring often. Pour off any fat.

2. Reduce the heat to medium. Stir the onion, pepper and cumin in the saucepan and cook until the vegetables are tender-crisp, stirring occasionally. Add the flour and cook and stir for 1 minute.

3. Add the picante sauce and broth and heat to a boil. Reduce the heat to low. Cook for 20 minutes or until the beef is cooked through and the mixture is thickened. Serve with the *Assorted Toppers*.

Makes 4 servings

Assorted Toppers: Shredded Cheddar cheese, chopped green onions and Pace® Chunky Salsa.

Prep Time: 20 minutes
Cook Time: 40 minutes

Black and White Chicken Chili

8 TYSON® Individually Frozen Boneless Skinless Chicken Breasts
1 large onion, chopped
2 jalapeño peppers,* seeded and finely chopped
1 tablespoon chopped garlic
2 cans (15 ounces each) Great Northern beans, undrained
2 cans (15 ounces each) black beans, drained
1 can (14 ounces) chicken broth
1 tablespoon chili powder
1½ teaspoons ground cumin
½ teaspoon salt

*Jalapeño peppers can sting and irritate the skin, so wear rubber gloves when handling peppers and do not touch your eyes.

1. Cut chicken into ½-inch cubes.

2. Coat large saucepan with nonstick cooking spray. Heat over medium-high heat. Add chicken; cook 3 minutes, stirring frequently. Add onion, jalapeños and garlic. Cook 7 minutes longer, stirring occasionally. Add remaining ingredients. Bring to a boil. Reduce heat; simmer, uncovered, 20 to 30 minutes or until chicken is done (internal temperature 170°F).

Makes 10 servings

Serving Suggestion: Top individual servings of chili with sour cream. Serve with a mixed green salad and hot tortillas or tortilla chips. You may freeze the chili in tightly sealed nonmetallic containers or freezer bags.

Prep Time: 10 minutes
Cook Time: 40 minutes
Total Time: 50 minutes

Lentil Chili

1 tablespoon canola oil
4 cloves garlic, minced
1 tablespoon chili powder
1 package (32 ounces) reduced-sodium vegetable broth
¾ cup dried brown or green lentils, rinsed and sorted
2 teaspoons smoked chipotle hot pepper sauce
2 cups peeled and diced butternut squash
1 can (about 14 ounces) diced tomatoes
½ cup chopped fresh cilantro
¼ cup pepitas (pumpkin seeds) (optional)

1. Heat oil in large saucepan over medium heat. Add garlic; cook and stir 1 minute. Stir in chili powder; cook and stir 30 seconds.

2. Add broth, lentils and hot pepper sauce; bring to a boil over high heat. Reduce heat to low; simmer 15 minutes. Stir in squash and tomatoes; simmer 18 to 20 minutes or until lentils and squash are tender.

3. Ladle into bowls; top with cilantro and pepitas, if desired.

Makes 4 servings

Turkey Vegetable Chili Mac

³⁄₄ **pound ground turkey**
 1 **can (about 15 ounces) black beans, rinsed and drained**
 1 **can (about 14 ounces) Mexican-style diced tomatoes**
 1 **can (about 14 ounces) diced tomatoes**
 1 **cup frozen corn**
½ **cup chopped onion**
 2 **cloves garlic, minced**
 1 **teaspoon Mexican seasoning**
½ **cup uncooked elbow macaroni**
⅓ **cup sour cream**

Slow Cooker Directions

1. Spray large nonstick skillet with nonstick cooking spray; heat over medium-high heat. Add turkey; cook and stir 5 minutes or until cooked through. Transfer to slow cooker. Add beans, tomatoes, corn, onion, garlic and Mexican seasoning. Cover; cook on LOW 4 to 5 hours.

2. Stir in macaroni. Cover; cook 10 minutes. Stir. Cover; cook 20 to 30 minutes or until macaroni is tender. Serve with sour cream.

Makes 6 servings

Tip: Feel free to substitute 2 ounces of any other pasta. Short pasta shapes like cavatappi, penne or rigatoni can be added straight out of the package. Longer shapes such as linguine, fettuccine or spaghetti should be broken in halves or thirds before being stirred in so that all the pasta can be fully immersed in the sauce.

Hearty Chicken Chili

1 onion, finely chopped

1 jalapeño pepper,* minced

1 clove garlic, minced

1½ teaspoons chili powder

¾ teaspoon salt

½ teaspoon ground cumin

½ teaspoon dried oregano

½ teaspoon black pepper

¼ teaspoon red pepper flakes (optional)

1½ pounds boneless skinless chicken thighs, cut into 1-inch pieces

2 cans (about 15 ounces each) hominy, rinsed and drained

1 can (about 15 ounces) pinto beans, rinsed and drained

1 cup chicken broth

1 tablespoon all-purpose flour (optional)

Chopped fresh Italian parsley or cilantro (optional)

Jalapeño peppers can sting and irritate the skin, so wear rubber gloves when handling peppers and do not touch your eyes.

Slow Cooker Directions

1. Combine onion, jalapeño, garlic, chili powder, salt, cumin, oregano, black pepper and red pepper flakes, if desired, in slow cooker.

2. Add chicken, hominy, beans and broth; stir well to combine. Cover; cook on LOW 7 hours.

3. For thicker chili, stir 1 tablespoon flour into 3 tablespoons cooking liquid in small bowl. Stir into slow cooker. *Turn slow cooker to HIGH.* Cover; cook on HIGH 10 minutes or until thickened. Garnish with parsley.   *Makes 6 servings*

Prep Time: 15 minutes
Cook Time: 7 hours 10 minutes

Pork and Red Bean Chili

1 tablespoon canola or vegetable oil
1 pound pork tenderloin, cut into ½-inch chunks
4 cloves garlic, minced
2 teaspoons chili powder
1 can (about 14 ounces) fire-roasted diced tomatoes
¾ cup jalapeño salsa
1 can (about 15 ounces) red kidney beans, rinsed and drained
½ cup chopped fresh cilantro

1. Heat oil in large saucepan over medium heat. Add pork, garlic and chili powder; cook 4 minutes or until pork is browned on all sides, stirring occasionally.

2. Add tomatoes and salsa; bring to a boil over medium heat. Reduce heat; simmer 10 minutes or until pork is no longer pink in center.

3. Stir in beans; simmer 3 minutes or until heated through. Ladle into bowls; top with cilantro. *Makes 4 servings*

7-Ingredient Chili

2 pounds ground turkey
1 large onion, chopped (about 1 cup)
2 tablespoons chili powder
½ teaspoon ground cumin
3½ cups V8® 100% Vegetable Juice (Regular or Low Sodium)
1 small green pepper, chopped (about ½ cup)
2 cans (about 15 ounces each) kidney beans, rinsed and drained

1. Cook the turkey, onion, chili powder and cumin in a 4-quart saucepan over medium-high heat until the turkey is cooked through, stirring often.

2. Add the vegetable juice, pepper and beans to the saucepan and heat to a boil. Reduce the heat to low. Cover and cook for 15 minutes or until the vegetables are tender. *Makes 6 servings*

Prep Time: 10 minutes
Cook Time: 25 minutes

Chili Beef Express

1 pound ground beef (95% lean)
¼ teaspoon salt
¼ teaspoon pepper
1 can (15½ ounces) chili beans in chili sauce, undrained
1 can (14½ ounces) chili-style chunky tomatoes, undrained
1 cup frozen corn
2 tablespoons chopped fresh cilantro

1. Heat large nonstick skillet over medium heat until hot. Add ground beef; cook 8 to 10 minutes, breaking into ¾-inch crumbles and stirring occasionally. Remove from skillet with slotted spoon. Pour off drippings from skillet; return beef to skillet and season with salt and pepper.

2. Stir in beans, tomatoes and corn; bring to a boil. Reduce heat; cover and simmer 10 minutes. Sprinkle with cilantro before serving.

Makes 4 servings (about 1¼ cups each)

Cook's Tip: This recipe may be doubled; prepare in stockpot instead of skillet.

Cook's Tip: Cooking times are for fresh or thoroughly thawed ground beef. Ground beef should be cooked to an internal temperature of 160°F. Color is not a reliable indicator of ground beef doneness.

Prep and Cook Time: 25 minutes

Favorite recipe from **Courtesy The Beef Checkoff**

Simple Turkey Chili

1 pound ground turkey
1 small onion, chopped
1 can (28 ounces) diced tomatoes
1 can (about 15 ounces) black beans, rinsed and drained
1 can (about 15 ounces) chickpeas, rinsed and drained
1 can (about 15 ounces) kidney beans, rinsed and drained
1 can (6 ounces) tomato sauce
1 can (4 ounces) chopped green chiles
1 to 2 tablespoons chili powder

1. Cook turkey and onion in Dutch oven over medium-high heat until turkey is cooked through, stirring to break up turkey. Drain fat.

2. Stir in all remaining ingredients. Bring to a boil. Reduce heat; simmer about 20 minutes, stirring occasionally. *Makes 8 servings*

Serving Suggestion: Serve chili over split baked potatoes.

Arizona Pork Chili

1 tablespoon vegetable oil
1½ pounds boneless pork, cut into ¼-inch cubes
Salt and black pepper (optional)
1 can (15 ounces) black, pinto or kidney beans, drained
1 can (14½ ounces) DEL MONTE® Diced Tomatoes with Onion & Garlic, undrained
1 can (4 ounces) diced green chiles, drained
1 teaspoon ground cumin
Tortillas and sour cream (optional)

1. Heat oil in large skillet over medium-high heat. Add pork; cook until browned. Season with salt and pepper to taste, if desired.

2. Add beans, tomatoes, chiles and cumin. Simmer 10 minutes, stirring occasionally. Serve with tortillas and sour cream, if desired.
Makes 6 servings

Prep Time: 10 minutes
Cook Time: 25 minutes

Spicy Verde Chicken & Bean Chili

> 2 tablespoons butter
> 1 large onion, chopped (about 1 cup)
> ¼ teaspoon garlic powder or 1 clove garlic, minced
> 1 tablespoon all-purpose flour
> 2 cups SWANSON® Chicken Stock
> 2 cups shredded cooked chicken
> 1 can (about 15 ounces) small white beans, undrained
> 1 can (4 ounces) chopped green chiles, drained
> 1 teaspoon ground cumin
> 1 teaspoon jalapeño hot pepper sauce
> 6 flour tortillas (8-inch), warmed
> Shredded Monterey Jack cheese
> Chopped fresh cilantro leaves (optional)

1. Heat the butter in a 12-inch skillet over medium heat. Add the onion and garlic powder. Cook and stir until the onion is tender.

2. Stir the flour into the skillet. Cook and stir for 2 minutes. Gradually stir in the stock. Cook and stir until the mixture boils and thickens.

3. Stir in the chicken, beans, chiles, cumin and hot sauce. Heat to a boil. Reduce the heat to low. Cook for 20 minutes, stirring occasionally.

4. Line **each** of **6** serving bowls with the tortillas. Divide the chili among the bowls. Serve topped with cheese and cilantro, if desired.

Makes 6 servings

Prep Time: 10 minutes
Cook Time: 40 minutes
Total Time: 50 minutes

Beef and Black Bean Chili

1 tablespoon vegetable oil
1 pound boneless beef round steak, cut into 1-inch cubes
1 package (14 ounces) frozen bell pepper and onion mixture
1 can (about 15 ounces) black beans, rinsed and drained
1 can (about 14 ounces) fire-roasted diced tomatoes
2 tablespoons chili powder
1 tablespoon minced garlic
2 teaspoons ground cumin
$\frac{1}{2}$ ounce semisweet chocolate, chopped
2 cups hot cooked rice
   Shredded Cheddar cheese (optional)

Slow Cooker Directions

1. Heat oil in large skillet over medium-high heat. Add beef; cook 5 minutes or until browned on all sides, turning occasionally. Transfer to slow cooker.

2. Stir in bell pepper and onion mixture, beans, tomatoes, chili powder, garlic and cumin. Cover; cook on LOW 8 to 9 hours.

3. Turn off heat and stir in chocolate until melted. Serve over rice and garnish with cheese.   *Makes 4 servings*

Head-'Em-Off-at-the-Pass White Chili

 1 tablespoon olive oil
 ½ cup chopped onion
 2 cans (15 ounces each) cannellini beans, undrained
 1 jar (11 ounces) NEWMAN'S OWN® Bandito Salsa, divided
1½ cups chopped cooked chicken
 ½ cup chicken broth
 1 teaspoon oregano leaves
 ½ teaspoon celery salt
1½ cups (6 ounces) shredded mozzarella cheese, divided

Heat oil in 2-quart saucepan; add onion and cook and stir until tender. Stir in beans, ½ cup of Newman's Own® Bandito Salsa, chicken, chicken broth, oregano and celery salt. Cover; simmer over medium heat 10 minutes, stirring occasionally. Just before serving, stir in 1 cup of mozzarella cheese. Divide chili evenly among serving bowls. Top each with a portion of remaining mozzarella and salsa.   *Makes 4 servings*

Acknowledgments

The publisher would like to thank the companies and organizations listed below for the use of their recipes and photographs in this publication.

The Beef Checkoff

Campbell Soup Company

Del Monte Foods

Newman's Own, Inc.®

Sargento® Foods Inc.

Tyson Foods, Inc.